I HAVE TO TELL YOU SOMETHING

I HAVE TO TELL YOU SOMETHING

BY ZARA BAS

I Have to Tell You Something by Zara Bas

ISBN: 9798814324900

Published by Zara Bas

www.goodthingsarewaiting.com

Dearest reader, these words were written to give you a space to untangle the strings of your heart.

Contents

SOFT TRUTHS

You can always start again. Clean out your social media. Create a new account for your new taste in music. Study or work in a new city. Start socialising with new people. Choose a new signature scent and style and purge the outdated parts of yourself.

If you don't like where you're at
but you don't know what to do about it

try starting again.

I Have to Tell You Something

Your wings are still hardening
gossamer strands of silk cradling you
transforming with the passing of time
but you're hesitant to emerge
from the safety of your chrysalis
and that is okay

You're not obligated to share pieces of yourself
that you are not yet ready to put on display.

All of you is welcome
even the parts you feel are too ugly to reveal
the parts that make your cheeks
glow red with embarrassment
the pieces you take great pains to conceal
you don't have to suffocate them anymore

All of you is welcome here.

You don't need to downplay who you are
stand confidently in your space
you are not an impostor in this space
you are meant to be here
your knowledge, skills and talent
are beyond your comprehension
but others see it

We all see it.

You have been told things about you
in the heat of the moment
that simply are not true
I know how they sting
how difficult they are to forget
they have been burned
and branded on your thoughts
but you are not the things they said to you
in the throes of anger.

I Have to Tell You Something

Let your art be clunky and awkward
let your creativity flow until it runs dry
regardless of how embarrassing
or unpleasant the product of it may seem
create for the sake of shifting stagnant energy
to something outside of yourself

The way you transmute
and alchemise your internal world
doesn't need to be flawless to be art
it doesn't need to be tweaked and edited
until it's 'good enough'
leave it unfinished if you want to
and enjoy the process of making something
without a bigger purpose.

Regardless of whether you believe it or not
you are important
you are worthy
you are good enough
you are acceptable
you are valuable

Those who are meant for you recognise it
and those who don't recognise it are not meant for
you.

Lovely promises to make yourself:

to stand by your side
when the rest of the world doesn't
to cherish your essence
and hold tightly to your sparkle
to love every little bit of your being
mercurial and wild
to listen and give words
to the sentiments within your heart.

You make
people feel
so understood.

Don't you think
you deserve
a little understanding too?

Emotional pain doesn't control you
it is only energy
allow it to flow through your body freely
without getting stuck in it
allow it to stay as long as it wants

Allow it to leave when it's ready.

It's human
that urge to escape to a cottage in the forest
desiring nothing more than to erase
each digital trace of you
from a chronically online culture

And when that hunger
insidiously sneaks up on you
I hope you listen to your hearts yearning
for all things slow
soft
simple.

Who you are is someone worth loving
not only for the way you make others feel
the way you show kindness
enlivening the days of strangers
and loved ones alike
who you are is someone worth loving

Simply as you are.

Healing doesn't just happen in the time spent meditating on recovery. It continues in the small moments. The time you and your sister spend applying face masks and you forget for a moment that there is healing to be done. Or when you catch the fragrance of spring on the air, infatuated with the signs of new life breaking through sun-warmed soil around you.

Soon you will see that the world is conspiring in every way possible to help you in your journey. And even when you don't realise it you are getting there.

Offer yourself patience
in places where
memories still bleed.

I Have to Tell You Something

I know you've been told the very opposite
but hear me out

you are worth the hassle
you are worth the inconvenience
you are not exasperating
you're not causing a fuss
asking for what you need is not being difficult

Stop apologising for being human.

Just like the sun,
when the moon takes it's place

You deserve time to recharge
to pause
to rest.

Honestly, all of this healing, setting
boundaries, learning about your needs stuff
takes so much practice. There will be many
times you'll fall back into old habits, setting
your needs aside and sacrificing your
boundaries. You'll look back and think about
how you missed an opportunity to practice,
but even becoming aware of those moments
after-the-fact is progress.

You will
find a love
that calms
your soul.

I don't know if I'm doing this correctly
this whole
'making a life for yourself' thing
but I am trying
and that is what matters.

The world wants to fit you
into neat little categories
it'll push you to pick
an area of expertise
a personality
a gender
it's okay if you don't want to pigeonhole
yourself into set spaces

You're a human being, not something to be
catalogued.

You love so deeply
and yes
sometimes it burns
but it is also impossibly beautiful
being capable of such full-bodied
celestial emotion.

People love you most
in your rawest state
with your clumsily
and imperfectly expressed
string-of-consciousness thoughts
the unabashed excitement you betray
before it's replaced with a stoic mask
you don't realise how charming you are

As your most undefended self.

And throughout your search
it seems you may have overlooked one
important fact

You were the answer all along.

I Have to Tell You Something

Loving you comes naturally
which does not mean it's always easy

No.

Loving you requires effort and time
sensitivity and understanding
loving you takes listening
to the subtext in your answer
it takes a perceptive eye to notice the minute
but distinct way your expressions
give away how you feel
loving you is not always effortless
but it is instinctive

And it sure is worth it

If you're lucky
you will go through a period of deep loneliness
and it will hurt at first
but in loneliness you will meet yourself
deeper than you could have imagined.

So then be basic
like what everyone else likes
enjoy the pumpkin spice lattes
wear leggings as pants
because no matter how mainstream

If you like it, you like it and that's a good enough
reason.

I know how it aches. Your stomach is in knots and no matter how many times you roll to the other side, you can't fall asleep. I know you've spent the night rubbing your temples in hopes it will ease the post-cry headache. I know how you tried to breathe through it, but you can't shake the feeling of the brick on your chest. And let me tell you - it doesn't last forever. Tomorrow the sun will rise and you will feel okay. The worries of the night will dissolve in morning clarity.

And you will feel alright again,
that I can promise you.

Because that's what love does
it makes it easier to breathe

That's what you did for me.

I hope you know
you are the reason for so many smiles
you bring so much happiness and joy
and you don't even notice it
you have lit up people's days
simply by being here.

It wasn't that you were hard to love
they just weren't capable of loving you
the way you deserved.

I hope yours is not a love
you have to struggle for
no ceaseless suffering
no begging for the bare minimum

I hope yours is a love that comes easily.

You are not a project awaiting completion
you are an ongoing masterpiece

learning

changing

evolving.

I Have to Tell You Something

When your body shakes with sorrow
and tears form a torrential downpour
know that someday soon
you will laugh until your sides hurt
you will smile until the corners of your mouth
can't take it any longer
and you will love
like you never thought possible.

I Have to Tell You Something

You are not a vessel
for other people's pain and hurt
you're a mirror for where they need to heal

not a container for their broken pieces.

You don't see yourself
when you stick your tongue out
and scrunch your nose
when you're compelled to silly dances
in the kitchen
if only you could see these moments
when you're most beautiful

You'd never question it again.

Trauma didn't make you stronger

You did that.

No matter how much they pressure you
there is no correct way to grieve
it's okay to still ache for things in the past
it's okay to move on in your own time
loss is a phenomenon
we all experience differently
and there's nothing wrong
with the way you're getting through it.

You are
going to build
a beautiful life for yourself.

When you start to heal
you start trying new things
you put yourself out there
to experience things you always wanted to
but were afraid to strive for
you expand your friendships
career goals
interests
when you start healing

lean into all the incandescent new growth.

They sold you
an illusion
having yourself all 'figured out'
as if you were
as simple as an equation.

I Have to Tell You Something

You are milk and honey
peaches and mango nectar
you are soft raindrops
and the ring of the high notes on a piano
you are the sun-dusted mid-afternoon moon
on a clear day
dew drops on frost-bitten grass
and the sparkle of new snow

how dare you let anyone treat you like dirt.

It's not just okay to be sensitive
it's beautiful to be sensitive
it's beautiful to be aware and feel deeply
it's beautiful to love with your heart
on your sleeve
don't admire the way they feel nothing

Your ability to feel is your strength.

I Have to Tell You Something

It comes back
the sparkle in your eyes
the curve of your smile
in time
it returns.

One day you're going to kiss the love of your life goodnight after a day of mundane activities like grocery shopping and napping, but you're going to feel soft and at peace inside because you get to do those things with your best friend.

You'll realise that the version of you that said you would never love again is gone, because now you look forward to the days you get to be here, loving someone fully and receiving the love you always deserved.

You once measured yourself in grades
numbers on scales
in certificates
now look at you

*You no longer need a unit of measurement to know
your value.*

I Have to Tell You Something

You had no one to run to back then
your little arms outstretched
waiting for someone to scoop you up
to pour love into you.

You were left on a wild and unforgiving sea
no life jacket, no far off island
or passing ship in sight
and now you still feel
the yearning for connection
your arms stuck searching
for an embrace that should have come
long ago.

But this time you're not alone
you, full of motherly tenderness, are here
stroking the picture of your younger self
curled up in your lap
wiping away the tears.

There is no lost love
in one way or another
love will always find it's way
back to you
maybe not in the same form
nor the same person
but love moves cyclically
back to it's giver
so love without abandon
with the blanket of comfort
that it will return

warmer
deeper
and softer.

I Have to Tell You Something

So I bravely choose
to put my fragile heart
in your hands
knowing you could drop it
but trusting that I
can pick up the pieces
if you do.

You don't need to prove you're hurting
for your pain to be real.

You do have what it takes
what it takes to get through this
what it takes to transcend
to become
to flourish
no matter how dark it gets

You have what it takes.

You,
with your sunny disposition
and tender heart,

have always been enough.

It's time to accept yourself
time to stop nitpicking
at every little part
that doesn't fit the impossible standard
the world set for you
it's time to embrace the imperfections
the rejections
the shame

Self-esteem comes when you accept all the
spaces in which you were made to feel
unworthy.

You're probably wondering whether what you experienced was really 'that bad?'. Let me tell you - If you have to question it, if it hurts, if it still runs through your mind, it was.

You don't have to feel guilty over the pain you're feeling.

I Have to Tell You Something

I wish you loud uncontrollable laughter
and smiles that make your eyes crease
I wish you messy hugs with drunk friends
and the warmth of a strangers kindness
I wish you red hot passion for the things
that make you happy
and 'I love you's from the people who matter.

Stay soft in the face of callousness
choose a full heart over heartlessness
be a beacon of tenderness
where insensitivity cannot thrive

No one can take your warmth from you.

I Have to Tell You Something

You might miss them right now
but I promise you
this feeling has an expiration date

One day you will meet someone
who fills your heart
full of a light
you couldn't find anywhere else
and you will understand
why this had to work out the way it has.

I Have to Tell You Something

To trust again
is my greatest battle
and I will win.

You know that moment when you're in the
bathtub.
When you put your head underwater and you
can hear your heartbeat?
Imagine that's how hard your heart is working
at all times

Your body loves you and wants to keep you here.

You deserve more than half-hearted love
more than uncertainty
you deserve a feast
not crumbs of affection.

HARD TRUTHS

Like a moth to a flame
we are drawn to others
who enter into a cycle of recreating past pains
playing bumper cars with each other's traumas

*Your greatest opportunity to heal lies in disturbing
the cycle.*

Your feelings are valid, but they are also fickle. One minute you'll be enamoured and the next you'll be enraged. In both of those moments you will feel that you absolutely must do something about it. Sometimes it's helpful - the push we need to change our course and abandon paths we've outgrown. But if you let every one of your feelings dictate your actions, you might miss out on the peace of stability. No matter the situation, there will always be moments of emotional turbulence. It is your decision whether to act on them or not.

You may never receive
the closure you needed from them
they might not give you
the apology or explanation you want

But the beauty of closure
is that it is entirely within your control
to create it for yourself.

I was scared
that if I said what I was thinking
it would shatter everything.

You might have missed
the little ways they love you.

You didn't notice
they filled your cup with more water
the tickets from the movies
they saved as a memory
were brushed off by you
as scrap pieces of receipts
they waited to watch you leave safely
but you left without looking back

If you look a little harder
you might realise they were loving you
all along.

I know you see the person they could be
you see the best in everyone
but you have to start seeing who they are now.

You have to keep going
you have to keep creating
keep trying
keep loving
keep believing
when it feels like no one's listening
and it doesn't seem to be going anywhere
when you want to throw the towel in
you have to keep going

You owe yourself at least one more chance.

Pretending I don't care
hurts more
than admitting I do.

Intellectualising your pain and feeling it
are two entirely different beasts
just because you understand what's happening
and why it's happening
doesn't make it hurt any less
logic and reason don't quell the sting of feeling

Only through the discomfort
of allowing ourselves to ache
does it ever truly dissipate.

They say that when you know
you know
but they forget

*Some of us have learnt to question everything to
survive.*

Maybe a good love is actually very mundane.
Maybe it's not the constant fire of blue-burning
flames books will have us believe it is.
Maybe it's just saying 'Look at this' at every
day objects and happenings and knowing
you're sharing in the mundane together.

The feeling of stillness in your heart from a
very average life made a little less average by
the one you love.

Sometimes your heart will hurt
and you won't know why
you will feel the need
to find an answer
but there simply may not be one

*Make peace with the idea that you can ache without
reason.*

It took us so long to build
and just seconds to break.

When you grow up in a home that perpetually feels like it's on fire, you develop a watchful eye for even the slightest hint of danger. The tragedy is that you may leave that home, but your hyper vigilance comes along with you. So when you find a space that is truly secure, you search so hard for signs of threat that you miss all the clues of peace. You don't recognise the feeling of safety.

Retrain your eye to focus on calm, comfort and contentment and you will begin to see it all around.

There are some pieces of you
that may never be fully understood
by anyone but yourself.

If you don't take care of your brain
it'll show up in your body
if you don't confront your needs
your body will confront them for you
if you don't respect your own limits
your body will force you to respect them.

It's scary to put your heart
in someone else's hands
to open every tender part of yourself
to another
but it's scarier to keep it locked away
never allowing your shadows
the chance to be loved.

I Have to Tell You Something

Your anger is nothing to be ashamed of
it is you loving yourself enough to say

I won't stand for this.

I know you want to rescue the ones you love
that's just who you are
you're the day-saver
the middle-of-the-night-phone-call friend
the drop-everything-if-you-need-it type
but it's not your job to fix it all

You deserve more than the position of emotional handyman.

When you prioritise the needs of others
over your own
you abandon yourself.

Shame gets displaced from person to person. Your parents' shame about their body, becomes your body-image difficulties. Your grandparents' shame around their status, becomes your compulsion to collect ever higher-ranking successes. But you were not put here to carry the shame of others. Before you were burdened with the weight of it, you were your own. It's time you returned to yourself.

You were there
until I needed you to be there.

I Have to Tell You Something

Waving your arms
in search of someone else
to come soothe you
every time discomfort hits
keeps you from learning
how to comfort yourself.

I wanted you to say
so much more than you did.

Let yourself feel. Cry in the shower if you need
to. Stare in silence at the ceiling. Scrunch up
like a paper ball. Claw at the ache in your chest
if it helps. But let yourself feel it all, because
that is not weakness. That's you being brave
enough to release a pain that would be so
much easier to ignore.

Yours is the most frightening love
not because you hurt me
but because you're the only one who hasn't.

If you keep everyone out
love can't get in.

It never feels like it
but the more you break down
the more you let the tears out
the more you let go enough to feel whatever
comes up for you

The more you heal.

Resentment grows when needs are left unsaid
instead of staying quiet
and letting bitterness fester
open your heart
express your desires
give others the opportunity to hear you
before you discount them.

I Have to Tell You Something

They'll tell you to 'shake it off'
as if you can reach into your organs
and rip the pain out of your chest
like the cells of your body
aren't buzzing with missing them
they'll nudge you with phrases like
'You were too good for them anyways'

But you can grieve someone
who wasn't good for you
you can grieve someone
who didn't treat you well.

Maybe it's time to take a step back
and see where you're making excuses
for them.

While you are changing, while you are growing - keep in mind that some people don't want to recognise the new aspects of yourself. Some people don't want to change their opinion of you, or work to rebuild their mental image of you. That's okay, keep growing for you, regardless of whether others acknowledge it or not.

Learn the difference
between being loved as a person
and being loved as a concept.

You hope that if you turn away
that the pain will disappear like smoke
but you do yourself a disservice
when you bury your hurt in a box to dust over
to take up space in a forgotten draw
somewhere in the catacombs of your mind
leaving it to fester

Pull up your pain like weeds
plant something beautiful in it's place.

You must be careful
to avoid framing new characters
as old villains.

I Have to Tell You Something

The truth is that some loves are temporary
some loves you will outgrow
some loves are lessons to learn
some loves are momentary
some loves won't be enough

And every time it will sting
you will think you'll never love again
but you will

You will love again and one of these times it will be
forever.

You were not put on this earth
to turn your life into a performance piece
for the judgment of others.

I hope you have the wisdom to see
that some of the worst monsters
pretend to live in the light
be fierce and unrelenting
with your self worth
to keep them far away
from your precious heart.

In a perfect world
I would never hurt you
and you would never hurt me
but as our traumas spill out onto each other
and wither away at our bones
I'm reminded we do not live in a perfect world

I must accept the fact that love is not perfect
and getting hurt is, at times, inevitable.

Sometimes you don't get what you want
because you deserve better.

Failure is a guarantee
irrespective of the effort you put in
or the quality of your work
at one point or another
you will come up against failure
but this doesn't make your pursuit
any less worthy

*Failure is an indication that you were brave enough
to try.*

That's how we heal
we keep going despite the fear.

In spite of it.

Yeah they're cute, but do they:

Respect you?
Do they value you?
Are they capable of deep empathy and
communication?
Do they seek to understand?
Are they working towards loving themselves?
Are they a positive influence on your life?
Do they support you and your decisions?
Do they take actions to show they care?
Would they stick by your side during a crisis?

Maybe all along your purpose
was simply to be
to feel
to laugh
to embrace
and just be.

Sometimes the best response
is to observe in silence.

The high of finding places to fix
within yourself
can quickly become another addiction
in the healing rat race
so don't forget

You can be flawed and still be flourishing.

One day you will look back
on pictures of yourself
and wonder why you curled your lip
with dissatisfaction
when you saw yourself in the mirror.

I wish you were my first love. If you were, I wouldn't be constantly waiting for the other shoe to drop. I wouldn't search for malice in your clearly pure intentions. If you were my first love, I would have no difficulties giving you every part of me. Loving you without abandon. I would have only known love as velvety and light.

Not for the inky, black-hearted and treacherous affair it can be.

The cost of not being true to yourself
for the sake of approval
is losing your authenticity
and that's a price
far too high to pay.

Learning to set boundaries comes with so
much anxiety. Anxiety over confrontation, the
other person's reaction, potentially losing them
and yet it is so necessary for healing.

Make some space for that anxiety and allow it
to exist, but continue setting your boundaries
in the face of it.

I Have to Tell You Something

You want everyone to like you
but do you like you?

As uncomfortable as it is to hear
sometimes you're the bad guy
the unhealthy one

Sometime's it's you.

I know change is tough
all you want to do
is wrap a comfortable blanket
of frozen time around you
a time of consistency
of rhythm
of routine

But just remember
change will bring with it
new growth and beauty
while killing off
the old and dead parts of yourself.

You shouldn't have
to put in
effort for two.

It's a Sunday night
and you've spent
the whole day
surrounded by people
and yet
you couldn't feel more alone

And that feeling only makes you human.

I Have to Tell You Something

You were oil
and I was water
repelled from ever fully holding you
little did I know
our molecular incompatibilities
saved me.

In the end, you'll walk away
and that will be the beginning.

Thank you, from the bottom of my heart to yours, for supporting my passion to write. I hope these words rested gently on your spirit. Please consider sharing this book with friends and family and leaving a review.

Reviews are the lifeblood of my writing and I would truly appreciate your thoughts on it.

To leave a review, within your Amazon account click 'Returns and Orders' > Write a product review or visit the link from which you brought this book and click 'write a customer review'

Manufactured by Amazon.ca
Bolton, ON

28490777R00074